The Pocket Guide: The Three Keys to Project Success

Dr. Markeith L. Porter

ISBN: **153554791X**
ISBN 13: **9781535547918**
LCCN Imprint Name: **City and State (If applicable)**

Avail a Leadership Style

Adept Planning

Adaptation to Change

By Dr. Markeith L. Porter

Contents

Introduction

This pocket guide is predicated on the fact that I have learned so much from working projects over a thirty-year career. The guide will describe the triple A's of project management that begin with making yourself *available* to a leadership style, being *adept* at planning, and *adapting* to situations. These three concepts will be the basis by which I bring about a plan to enhance your ability to *ace* your project no matter what level of experience you have. A good foundational knowledge of the concepts in this book can make you both successful on the job and in life. I often look back on my thirty years of experience in working projects in the United States Navy and as a civilian working three million to sixty-million-dollar projects.

A teacher once taught me the five P's of life: proper planning prevents poor performance. This concept has helped guide me in obtaining a doctorate. My wish is that you use the concept of the triple A's in project management to help guide you to the success you desire from any project that you undertake.

Avail a Leadership Style

First, leadership to me is the ability to guide one to a specific result rather than by direct or influential energy. In leadership, there are several styles: pacesetter, affiliative, directive, visionary, and coaching.

The pacesetter has a do-it-or-I-will-do-it-for-you mentality. The directive is "do it the way I told you or else." The affiliative will do it with as little strife as possible, most of the time looking for harmony. The visionary has the big picture in mind and normally has the long-term direction. Finally, coaching normally focuses on the long-term development of others (Dulewicz and Higgs 2016).

The pacesetter in the race is a good leadership style in that it provides a direct example of how to get the job done. Fallback on this leadership style happens when you become tired. If there is significant tasking the pacesetter may slow down, allowing the deadline to fall behind.

The directive leadership style can be cumbersome in that the leader tells you to do a task, but he has no skill or knowledge of what is wanted or required. "Do it or else" will get you only so far before a breakdown in communication causes the project to go awry.

Coaching is a great leadership style in that one can meet the goal with little or no direction except when the worker is new to the task. Coaching may take an extraordinary amount of time for development depending on the person's ability to grasp complex and sometimes simple concepts (Dulewicz and Higgs 2016).

Affiliative is a good concept for groups that are very familiar with one another. Normally they have coffee and donuts and talk with one another outside of the project. However, when a new person happens along, they can be very resistant to that person and often make tasking more difficult either on purpose or not.

Visionary leadership is a long-term approach. Setting milestones along the way can help develop confidence in employees. Communication and direction become clearer as the end nears. One must develop a mission and have strategies that can enhance long-term success. The problem with this method of leadership is getting others to buy into your vision. Do they see themselves as part of the future or suspect they will be eliminated? For instance, computers provide efficiency; computers enhance the employee's ability to complete the job correctly the first time. However, computers have the added ability to eliminate jobs, allowing the company to do more with less.

Each of the leadership styles listed can come into play. When you have an abundant dose of one particular style, the project can stall and eventually become unsuccessful. Why talk about leadership styles? What can come from this? A person can know and understand what leadership characteristics he or she needs to develop. When one leadership style is not working, you may employ another. Some goals are reached by pacesetting and others may be reached by directive.

This pocket guide has two concepts of special interest: project failure and project success.

Project managers, in the interest of the customer, must be able to define project failure. Testing is one sure-fire way of defining success and failure. When we look at project failure, we start with a lack of user involvement. This has proved fatal to many projects. Lack of senior management involvement in the project often affects priorities and resources such as budget and staffing. If management does not feel the project is worth continuing to commit funds and people to, it normally withdraws and accepts losses.

The next failure is long timescales. When the project's timescales are really long, it is important to divide the project into separate deliverables. This gives the project some short-term goals and keeps the team interested in the project.

The next failure is poor delineated requirements. Projects with vague requirements often lead to scope creep. In this situation, the project manager has not defined the project deliverables at the onset of the project. Normally, the project manager builds what he or she thinks is needed, not what is in the drawings and specification. Users must know what they want and be able to specify it precisely (Cerpa and Verner 2009).

The next failure is no change-control system. Knowing your requirements and understanding what is to be delivered are important. If there is a change, it must be in writing and version two, three, four, etcetera must be assigned. Each change must be annotated in the drawing and written so that when it comes to testing, the desired results are reached.

The last failure is poor testing. If many testing requirements are missing and no methodical, this can lead to inadequate time to perform tests because the project is late.

The second concept that must be addressed is defining project success. The use of acceptance testing should in part build confidence in the users. Personnel should be adequately trained and should have well-designed testing requirements to achieve the testing objectives. On the surface, you might think that defining success would be relatively simple, but in practice, different people define success in different ways. Based on discussions with a wide variety of project participants and observation of people's actual behaviors in real-life projects, I've classified the different definitions as such: The project is a success if it delivers on all agreed-upon project objectives, be they based on scope, schedule, budget, quality, or outcomes (Goatham, 2016).

Adept Planning

Adept planning starts with documentation, which contains many different variables. Variable one is the statement of work (SOW). The statement of work tells the project manager what job he needs to accomplish. For example, installing an air conditioner in a building four stories tall may call for many taskers. The base on which the foundation is to be mounted might be the first item of consideration. The statement of work should list in the drawing what is needed to accomplish the task. The drawing should contain electrical hookup, piping arrangements, testing procedure, structural procedure, painting or coating procedure, decking procedure, and machinist procedures. The statement of work should contain testing and operation publications. List any coding requirement or standards the air conditioner must meet.

The requirement section normally lists what is required of the laborer and project manager. This is normally listed in general terms. For example, the contractor should complete drawing number 22,477 in reference section two. The notes section should contain any special instructions. Such requirements ensure a dial is turned counterclockwise when starting timing procedures. A step such as this may be considered critical before operation can begin.

Material delivery and/or status are critical; one might not want to start the project until all materials are at hand. This may not be possible on all occasions. The reliability of the vendor in meeting critical dates can be taken into account. The project manager should be making this call. His or her experience in dealing with the vendor may be the only means of making this judgement. Long lead- time material is another judgment call. Be sure to get material on order as soon as funding is in place. Provide a document that lists every part on order, when it is due, and the date it arrived. On a weekly basis, the project manager should go through the list to determine priority. Divide material on a consumable verses safety verses operational basis.

Procurement management is another important aspect of project control. Reliable vendors can prevent the unnecessary cost of hiring inventory personnel. The advent of just-on-time suppliers can prevent having to do inventory. For example, if you need a bicycle wheel in two weeks, you can order the part from a vendor to have it delivered on the date required. No inventory is required. The part is on time. The bicycle is ready for delivery to the customer.

Adept planning begins with the most important aspect of project management: determining scope. The ability to write a clear scope statement may take some experience. But experienced or not, you must be able to determine scope because when the customer's expectations change, you need to delineate whether it is an actual deliverable.

Another variable of documentation is the schedule. The schedule is a complete list of taskers that ensures the job meets the statement of work and not people's expectations. Expectations change depending on the level in the chain of leadership. At the operator level, people are much more interested in the unit-level management. At the department division or department head level, they are concerned with system-level management. Finally, at the CEO or captain level, they are interested in the organization-level management.

With the schedule, organization is critical. Each task must be associated with a name of responsibility, a start date, and an end. How many hours will it take to complete? The task must have a priority listed along with whether the task is sequential, in conjunction with, or just a plain stand-alone. This section of planning may need your most adept planning requirements. The reason this is so important is because it is primarily due to experience. If you are undertaking a complex project and it has never been accomplished before, the planning may require some in-depth thinking. Aligning a tasker based on sequence is not so consequential if there is adequate time to complete a project. Most projects have a due date, and a due date will force one to know the items that can be completed in conjunction with the other. For instance, if you are drywalling, you cannot complete flooring in conjunction or simultaneously. However, if you are completing windows, there is no reason to stop you from laying your electrical cables.

Software

Choosing a software to run your project does make delineating who does what and when and where much faster. However, the same thought process must go into creating this documentation as the schedule does. The software, when completed with all the information listed above in the schedule, will make the job much easier to track. Ad hoc reports can be run on how much money has been spent on a weekly, monthly and quarterly basis.

Worker hours can be totaled on each task for future projects. One of the key components of software is the allocation of work hours. Say you assign work hours to a specific task, and you assign too many hours. For instance, changing a tire on a car may take two hours, and on the schedule, you only gave it thirty minutes. Your completion rate on the task has been overshot by one and half hours. This will create a skew in the report curve. The example provided in this small project does not affect much, but think in terms of a project that is six-months long and this was done repeatedly. Your curve and project will have a significant skew.

Now let us look at this from another point of view. For example, you put not enough hours on a task and gave yourself two hours of float. What is float? Float is when you have a task that you know will take thirty minutes to complete, but you give yourself two hours. In this case, you have one and a half hours of float. In this small example, float does not hurt, but if it's taken over a sixth month project, float can help in times when another task is taking longer than expected. It may decrease your amount of float but does not hurt the overall project. Float may have an adverse effect in that it may skew your project's projection to complete and budget. More experienced project managers would rather have the latter than the former mentioned. When using software to plan and manage your project, remember that software does not alleviate your responsibility to know and track your project.

Software also provides the project manager with the critical path to complete the project. A simplified example of critical-path project management (CPM) is this project plan for building a house. All the tasks in the project are listed in the work breakdown structure (WBS); then the dependencies between the tasks are determined, and the duration of each task is calculated.

Calculating the Critical Path

Most project-management software programs will calculate a CPM outline for you. If the project is complex, this may be necessary. For a simple case, like in the following paragraph, you can determine the critical path for yourself.

Start with the earliest task. Then see what tasks can't start until that one is finished. The longest of these tasks is the next task in the critical path. Figure out what tasks depend on completion of that second task, and then the longest of them becomes the third step in the critical path. Continue this until you reach the end of the project (Goatham 2016).

Documenting Milestones

A project milestone is a significant event in the project that may signify the acceptance or verification of completion of a project phase, task, decision, or deliverable. It is important to note that milestones are not work activities but rather significant events during the project that usually have a duration of zero. Milestones may be added to the project by the project sponsor or by the project team through the planning phase of the project. While a summary of project milestones should be included in the project charter, scope statement, and WBS dictionary, it is helpful to include a stand-alone milestone list as part of the project-plan documentation.

Most teams consist of a few experienced personal and some new to the project. If possible, pick those that can contribute positively to the project. New personnel will need more communication than those that have completed the operation many times. Picking the right team for a house may consist of an electrician, carpenter, mason, window installer, drywaller, plumber, painter, and insulator. As the project manager, you must know every member of the team's job and skill level. You must know the sequence by which each must participate. A simple word of advice: know your people. Know what makes them tick in order to get the most out of them.

Documented Procedures

Procedures are paramount to how we approach every task in project management. When we look at the trades that actually conduct the work, all have their own procedures they observe to get the job done. When completing the job or task, we want it complete but also done safely. (Later we will discuss a few safety precautions that cut across all trades.)

Take for instance a welder who installs a foundation on a ship. He or she has certain procedures and standards he or she must observe to install a foundation properly (without being presumptuous and thinking that I know every aspect of the welders' trade). I do know that he or she must pick any location on a given ship and take a paint sample to test the paint for heavy metals. He or she must remove any lagging material. (Lagging protects the steel wall from moisture.) He or she must remove the paint once results are received from the lab stating the paint has no heavy metals. Then with a level and precision ruler, he or she must measure out all low points to ensure the foundation is level once the welding begins. When welding is complete, he or she will then pass the foundation on to the machinist to ensure machining is complete, normally to get the foundation flat on top to some thousandth degrees. The process is complete depending on the amount of equipment cabinets to be installed.

There are many trades, such as electricians, deckers, laggers, pipefitters, carpenters, riggers, ship fitters, quality assurance, environmental, crane, sheet metal, and labor. Each trade has its own set of procedures and technical publications it must abide by.

For example, in the welding trade, welding procedures are annotated in the following.

- *Fabrication, Welding, and Inspection of Ships' Structure*

- *American Bureau of Shipping Rules for Building and Classing Steel Vessels*

- *Fabrication, Welding, and Inspection of Metal Boat and Craft Units*

- *Requirements for Welding and Brazing Procedures and Performance Qualifications*

- *Fabrication and Inspection of Brazed Piping Systems*

- *Requirements for Fabrication Welding and Inspection, and Casting Inspection and Repair for Machinery, Piping, and Pressure Vessels*

- *Welded Joint Design*

- *Nondestructive Testing Acceptance Criteria*

- *Requirements for Nondestructive Testing Methods*

- *Requirements for Repair and Straightening of Bronze Naval Ship Propellers*

- *Repair and Overhaul, Main Propulsion Boilers*

- *General Specifications for Overhaul of Surface Ships*

- *Repair, Welding, Weld Cladding, Straightening, and Cold Rolling of Main Propulsion Shafting*

- *Superstructure Cracking Repair/FFG7 Class, Ship Repair Manual*

- *AERMC, FFG7 Class Aluminum Deckhouse Critical Welds and Critical Weld Regions*

- *Technical Manual for CG-47 Class Superstructure Cracking Repair*

- *SERMC, Quality Assurance Requirements for Welding 5XXX Series Aluminum Structure for CG-47 Class*

As one can see, one trade may have several publications and procedures it must adhere to. As project manager, you are to make yourself familiar with the requirements to ensure quality is provided to the customer.

Communication

When you are a new project manager, you will have to familiarize yourself with a new language. Do not let the new language overwhelm you. Always revert to the common language everyone speaks in clear, precise statements and short and precise sentences that let the project team know exactly what is expected. In a small exercise I once had a part in, the narrator whispered, "I know why the caged bird sings," in the first person's ear. After going through ten people, it came out the other end "There is a blue bird in a cage." It is important that you know what you are trying to communicate, whom you are communicating to, and how and when you communicate.

Document Testing

Testing is unique in that testing has three levels: unit, subsystem, and system.

In the unit-level test, required tools consist of a multimeter, an oscilloscope, or maybe a megger. Each serves a specific purpose; the multimeter may be used to check resistance in a cable or voltage and current. The oscilloscope is used to measure frequency of a wave. The wave has some form of voltage. The system helps with setting timing in different circuit cards. The megger normally is used to check shielding in a cable. There are other unit testing, but hopefully I have provided a start.

The subsystem of functional testing is used to measure the workings on group components. In a particular system, the system may contain functional areas; take for instance a computer display. The computer has a power supply, a motherboard, a disc drive, and a video game card. The disc player may be taken out and tested on another computer to check to see if it works. If the disc player works in another system, it may be installed again in the original computer; this is a subsystem of the entire system. The system has to work overall. This means that all functional units work to engage the overall system test. This is the desired state.

This concept also works with a house. The stove is a unit in the house. The air conditioner maybe considered a functional area. The house is the complete system. Each must work for the overall comfortable living of the human that resides in the house. Testing should have a record of tracking each year when the gas is turned on in the winter. It should be checked for leaks, and a carbon-monoxide-alert unit should be checked to ensure safety.

Testing may be overlooked by some; to consider testing a loose-end deal is not giving the proper credence this step should have. Testing is a certifying step. If you buy a new cellular phone, you do not want to go home and then in turn it on only to have to bring the phone back because it does not work as expected. It is common for testing to become a human-error problem.

Adaptation to Change

The third and key factor to project success is adaptation. This corresponds to version and to what version of change you are on. When a new, unexperienced project manager is not adept at planning, someone has to make a decision. Do not be afraid to make a decision or push the button. Do what it takes to make the decision as informed as possible. Here is a bit of a speech I use to motivate myself to make a decision whether the decision is on a project or life.. You must remember that your plan is a living document. Every aspect of the project is subject to change. There should not be much change in the original statement of work. All items on your plan should be logged. If a tasker changes, you must log it in a lesson-learned folder or tablet. Try to take copious notes on any change. The key is to perform much better on your second attempt at the same project. On a new job, you want to lessen the amount of tutelage you need from more experienced project managers.

Change requires direction. The direction may be from e-mail, telephone, or word of mouth. Most people today require an e-mail to follow up on conversations. The key is not to have someone say, "I never got that word." When you hear this statement, it is often accompanied with "We may have made an error." This error may be simple, or it can be of a critical nature. Remember, it is your responsibility to see that the project is complete and on budget.

The one sure way to get fired is not completing the aforementioned and then getting someone hurt or killed on the job. There is a fine line between hurrying someone to complete a task and getting an individual hurt. One way to mitigate such circumstances is to have a safety brief prior to the project that is about to be accomplished. You want to make sure everyone's head is in the game, especially when conducting complex or dangerous operations.

Controlling pricing, timing, and schedule is critical. To ensure events are happening as they should, one might consider sending out notices the day or week before. This give the trade supervisor or leader time to ensure he or she is working the project. It is important to note that the leader of the trade may be working on other items he or she considers more of a priority. It is up to you to communicate your issues. Address the issues in a formal e-mail rather than going to his or her boss about things not going your way. Try not to bite the hand that feeds you. Only go to his or her boss as a last result.

Delegation is a very good time-management technique. It is very easy for a project manager to get mired down in all the tasks you have before you. Without trust in your people and a willingness to have them complete their tasks, you will never finish a project on time. With delegation, two other aspect of the project team aid in getting a job complete. Collaboration and teamwork during project planning is a key way to get off to a good start at a project's execution. Among the trades and project team, everyone needs to be willing to address issues that affect more than one trade. For instance, when deck work is taking place, no other trades can be performed in the vicinity of the work. However, if windows are being worked on, drywall and electrical-cable installers can be operating in the vicinity.

Responsibility

The project stakeholder has certain interests in the project. Depending on the position or title, the stakeholder affects the project in many different aspects. For instance, the project leader has the overall responsibility to get the job done in accordance with the scope, funding, and schedule. Project team members support the project by doing the actual labor. They are mostly referred to as the laborers. Senior management will authorize the funds and other resources for the project. Project customers will determine if the project satisfies the requirement listed in the scope. Ensure it is the requirements and not their expectations. Resource managers are considered your financial and production managers. They will determine budget and the level of experience your workers must have to be assigned to your project.

Completely staffing the project is akin to allocating resources to every activity; staffing, time, and funding are of much concern. The location and availability of more experienced talent is a great concern. Many take vacation during summer months and holidays. Try not to schedule key events during high-absent periods. Vendor flexibility is another must. If the project is slightly ahead or behind, the vendor must make himself or herself available. The suppliers are similar to staffing. Any material required must be affirmed with the fore mentioned principles.

Unplanned Events

Nature has a way of ruining projects. Earthquakes, hurricanes, and tornadoes are unplanned events in which not much planning can be mitigate. Rain and wind can be mitigated in small amounts. A simple tarp may allow work to continue if the project is outdoors. Ensure your budget can absorb the expense. Depending on the type of contract, mitigating these natural phenomena may be possible. Beware that these items are not planned into a project, but they may impact success or failure. Leadership may have to request an extension to the project if extensive damage occurs or if one or more of the unplanned events take place.

Project Risk

The ability to assess risk can prevent the project from derailing. Of course, you cannot always think of everything that might go wrong before a project starts. But mitigate as much risk as possible. Remember, hindsight is always twenty/twenty. When events do come up that were not expected, perform a risk assessment at the time. Always identify, assess, control, and evaluate the risks on a new task or tasks.

Equipment Tools

Equipment may require certain tools to complete a procedure. Take for instance aligning the propeller on a ship. The propeller will require a one-and-a-half-inch metric Allen wrench. This wrench is extremely rare, and the project manager may have to have the wrench fabricated.

Special tools are a control item. Once the tool is used to complete the operations it was design for, the tool is normally turned over to the customer or put in a rotary pool to be used on later projects. Special tools should be identified early in the planning stage and should be acquired as early as possible. Special tools are the most time-consuming item on a lead-time list, so identify them early and get them on order as soon as possible.

Environmental Concerns

Note early in the project those items that must be mitigated because of environmental concerns. Normally an agency regulates the work that we perform. A person that does decks on a ship must abide by OSHA standards. If any of the dust from removing the deck falls in the water, this may in turn cause a violation. The violation may be omitted and deemed a minor incident. The violation may lead to a fine and/or sanction against the company that created the violation. Having proper damage controls in place can cause the investigating agency to deem the problem minor with some small infraction. If prevention measures are totally disregarded, I do not know what can be used as an excuse. A more practical example is the tar used on houses to install roof shingles. The material must not be thrown in the garbage; it must be disposed of properly to prevent damage to the atmosphere.

Security

A major concern is security of your project. This may be as simple as a lock on a fence for the day or posting a guard. When classified material is concerned, the project may take on a new dimension. There are plenty of regulations involved in securing classified material. Take for instance if you as project manager have a drawing that has been deemed secret. You will only be able to view that drawing at work. Never take secret material home. The material will be required to be locked in a safe that has been slated as proper storage of secret material. Drawings, publications, and specifications that have not been deemed classified still require some level of security. When on your computer, it is OK to view material. Once complete, one should secure the computer, remove any authentication key card, and if leaving for the day, lock the computer and room.

Inspections

A daily inspection of the work or the worksite should be conducted. Items of concern should be your major focus. For instance, you get word the electrician installed a two-prong outlet and the drawing or specification states that it should be three pronged. This is a safety issue for the customer, and your professionalism should make you go back to the electrician and reinstall. Environmental issues should also be taken into account. One should frown on illegal items being dumped in the trash bins. A good walk through allows one to see exactly where the project is. One can then make projections one to a few steps ahead. Always keep in mind how each step fits into the next milestone or project completion.

Project Cost

The cost of a project is just as important as the project itself. Three costs that are associated with the project are cost estimation, budget, and cost control. Once estimation and budget are set, cost control is critical. The little things can eat away at project success. Take for instance a washer that is required to go on a bolt. The laborer decides not to put the washer on the bolt for some unknown reason. The inspector comes later on for quality assurance and says the washer has to be on the bolt for proper spacing. The whole job is complete and ready for testing. Now the system has to be reworked and shut down to install the washer, creating delays and rework that drive up cost. This type of situation presents itself all the time in project management. The key to mitigating this is training the laborer in quality assurance early in his or her arrival on the job.

Safety

Be sure to note that these safety items are not all inclusive; the ones listed are just enough to get one started. Safety is the one thing that project managers do not control, but they are held completely accountable for others' actions. Safety briefs are mandatory for all dangerous operations. They are design to keep the entire team's heads in the game. A roofer on the roof must wear the proper shoes for gripping. A janitor must wear a back brace to ensure he or she keeps his or her back straight while lifting. These operations may not seem to be very dangerous, but slips, trips, and falls account for over 37 percent of the reportable injuries in the United States. I have listed a few safety issues all managers should be aware of.

Back

- Bend your knees to lift a load.

- Use a brace to ensure your back remains stable during the lift.

- Use a two-man lift for items above fifty pounds.

Electrical

- The two-man rule applies when working on live electrical equipment.

- Use an electrical glove when measuring voltage.

- Ensure a safety glove is safety checked before use.

- Ensure you and your designated helper are both CPR qualified.

Crane

- Never stand under a lifted load.

- Ensure you listen for the whistle when a load is suspended in the air.

- Ensure you use designated walkways when transiting crane-lift areas.

Power Tools

- Ensure tools are electrical-safety checked.

- Never turn on the equipment and then plug in the equipment.

- Ensure electrical tools are grounded.

Slips, Trips, and Falls

- Ensure scaffolding is checked every day.

- Ensure nothing is left on the floor to trip on.

- Foot and knee knockers should be laced with florescent tape

- Holes should be covered to prevent falls.

- Watch your head for overhanging items.

- Always carry a flashlight, whistle, and florescent vest for long, dark areas.

Project Closure

The keys to unlocking project success are found in how well you study project failures. One should work to resolve the normal failures in projects early in the adept planning process. This can set your project on a solid foundation at a project's start. Understanding leadership roles and responsibilities are essential to project success. Having an ability to assess a project's needs and people is paramount in providing project accomplishment. The effort one puts forth to eliminate project failures in the planning phase will reduce the chance of failure. Adept planning must be instituted to ensure project execution goes off with as little changes as required. Finally, change in the project is inevitable. With the exception of scope, the project will change. Understanding issues that arise in the change process is a must for project managers. Documentation of change is a must, and the project manager must assess how the change will impact the project's milestones and completion.

References

Cerpa, N., and J. M. Verner. 2009. "Why Did Your Project Fail?" *Communications of the ACM*, 52 (12):, 130–134.

Dulewicz, V., and M. Higgs. 2005. Assessing Leadership Styles and Organizational Context. *"Journal of Managerial Psychology* 20 (2): 105–123.

"Why Projects Fail" Goatham, R. http://calleam.com/WTPF/?page_id=2213